Parenting

How to be a Great Parent and Raise Awesome Kids

By Patrick Baldwin

ACDAInc.Org

Special Request

Thank you for purchasing our book and supporting our Ministry. We have a Special Request for those that have purchased this book on the Kindle platform. We wanted to make you aware that Amazon's Kindle platform pays per pages "read". Our Special Request is that if you appreciate our Ministry's efforts to put out books such as this or if you would simply like to support our Ministry's work to please scroll to the back of the book, even if you don't "read" the book right away. This is how we will get paid through the paid per pages criteria.

We all lead such busy lives nowadays and can get side tracked so easily please take a moment to support us now by allowing us to be paid by scrolling to the end of the book – Then go back and read it at your leisure.

We deeply appreciate Your support and know that God will Bless You as You have Blessed this Ministry.

Dedication

This book is dedicated to my loving family who continues to be my inspiration and motivation. You have always encouraged me to follow my dreams and live with no regrets. You are eternally appreciated for all you have done and continue to do to enrich my life in so many ways.

This Book is also dedicated to you the reader and your family. I pray that this book will be a blessing to you as you read it.

God Bless.

Forward

There's nothing like being a parent. Parenting is the absolute greatest and most honorable job on earth. It's also the most difficult, terrifying, amazing, and most fulfilling job on earth. When it comes to raising kids most parents are eager to listen and learn from those who've been-there-done-that. We crave knowing what works and what doesn't when it comes to getting your baby to sleep through the night, potty training, homework, monitoring social media, setting rules and guidelines, and all those other parenting 'things'.

I want to suggest, however, that parenting is about much more than the things that have just been mentioned. Parenting is about teaching our children *who* to be and not just *what* to be. Or as I like to say, *"Parenting is being there; listening, talking, forgiving, asking forgiveness and most of all, loving with the same unconditional love we receive from Jesus."*

That's the reason for this book—to provide you with the encouragement and instruction necessary to raise up your children to be respectful, intelligent, confident, compassionate, responsible, and Godly people – You know, Awesome Kids!.

Each of the individual subject matters we're going to look at will address both the physical or tangible aspects and the intangible or emotional aspects of parenting.

So without further ado, let's get started. Let's get down to the joys of parenting with our best foot, heart, and mind forward.

Table of Contents

Chapter 1:

Don't Lie to Your Kids

Just like the chapter on sexuality, this chapter is going to be short and sweet. In fact, I could easily sum up the subject of lying to your children by simply saying, "Don't do it...not ever!" and be done. I'm actually tempted to do that, but me being me, I can't quite bring myself to do it. I want to expound on the subject of lying by saying the following...

There is no such thing as a good Lie

A lie is a lie is a lie. *To say it's just a little lie or a half-truth is like saying a woman is just a little bit pregnant. It's not possible.*

I know some of you are thinking about all those times when you've been asked "Did you get my birthday present yet?" or "Is there really a Santa Claus?" or "Who is the tooth fairy…really?" or "Did Fluffy go to heaven?"

When your little ones ask questions like this, rather than lying, you simply need to say, "I am the tooth fairy." Or "I don't know if Fluffy is in heaven but the Bible talks about animals in heaven so he might be. I'm sure if animals are in heaven Fluffy will be there, too."

Now were talking about Christmas, Easter or any other such holiday that there is some kind of supernatural character you want to let your child know right from the beginning that there is no such thing as Santa Claus, the Easter Bunny, the tooth fairy or any other such thing. Not some parents these things may be a tradition or commonplace and not even thought about.

However, it's important to start from the very beginning with a vow to yourself, to child and to God never to lie to one another. If you let your yes be yes and you know be no you'll do well.

The reason why this is of such a critical importance is because this is the foundation for building a great relationship with your child, not only now but also in the future when they become an adult. If you begin to lie to them even about something you may feel to be a harmless tradition such as Christmas and Santa Claus you are setting up yourself and your child for serious problems to come.

So let's walk through a scenario: for the first X amount of years you have if told and taught your child Santa is real and then through whatever means they find out that this is all been a lie, that their parent has lied to them for so many years – how do you think they are going to feel, what do you think this will do to your relationship?

Ultimately lies are the seeds of destruction for any relationship, especially one between children and their parents – guard your relationship with the ever present vigilance necessary to ensure its proper growth and development.

In my humble opinion it is better to be brutally honest than to cover a truth with a lie. That being said you have to talk with your children in a matter in which is age appropriate. You obviously don't want to traumatize your child by giving them more information about a given topic (whatever that topic is) than they can handle further age. My philosophy has always been a gradual increase philosophy with everything, and thus by the time that they are grown you have a well-balanced awesome kid, all grown up, but always your kid.

You'll notice I left the Santa question until last. That's because in my opinion, it is one that needs to be handled gently in order to help give children the capability to enjoy every aspect of the holiday season and to be respectful of the way parents of your children's peers choose to handle the situation. You have to be the guiding light and the source of truth for your child but do it in a manner that is age-appropriate and does not cause further confusion.

If you've already started traditions that have been based on a lie there is still time depending upon their age to undo the situation.

Don't just think because you've already established specific traditions that are based on lie that you should sit back and do nothing about it, assuming that in time they will understand. Well to that I say you are indeed correct, "In time they will definitely understand" but what they will understand is that their mother or father has lied to them. So my advice to you is to make a good-faith effort to rectify the situation, to rebuild potential trust that may have been lost in the past, and talk to your kids – have a conversation, a serious conversation with them (again age-appropriate) in which you promise each other moving forward that no matter what you will always tell them the truth.

Here is what I suggest for handling the "Santa question"…

- If your children already know about Santa and are trying to decide whether or not he is real, help them reason it out and come to the truth on their own or if age appropriate burst their bubble and tell them the whole thing is a hoax. Think of it like a Band-Aid – it's better to pull it off quickly than to try to do it slowly, painfully, step by painful step.

- You can do this by asking them:
  - How they think it would be possible for Santa to give every child gifts
  - How do they think Santa could travel the world in a few hours
  - Remind them that reindeer can't fly—that only birds can fly
  - Talk about the climate of the North Pole
  - Once they see the reasoning, be honest and tell them Santa is something that is made up.

- Remind them of the fact that Christmas is a time to celebrate Jesus' birth and that this aspect of Christmas should be first and foremost in our minds – Not Gifts

The same thing can apply for the Easter Bunny or any other character.

The fallacy of good lies also goes for those instances when someone asks questions like, "Do you like my outfit?" or similar questions like, "Am I gaining weight". In these instances we need to teach our children to not lie by saying something they don't mean. We as parents have to be prepared to receive truth just as much as we want to give truth to our kids. My grandma had a saying, "Don't ask me if you don't want to hear the truth". This very saying resonates with the core principle of never lying to your child. We have to teach our children to boldly speak their mind, to speak truth, to speak out against things when necessary and do it all with confidence, respect, tact, sincerity, and of course love.

We live in a society and a world in which massive amounts of individuals are hypersensitive and politically correct yet the truth is not a relative thing, the truth is absolute and there is no shades of gray in it.

Remember…being honest doesn't have to be harsh, rude, or tactless. You can be honest and polite at the same time. In fact I would say truth without politeness is in fact a lie for comes from hatred and the dishonest heart for truth in and of itself is never a rude thing. Politeness, manners, and respect are part of the key elements to the essence that makes us enlightened human beings and not mere animals.

The lies we tell our children to Tell

I know a mom who told her twelve year old daughter to lie to her dad about how much something cost. Mom didn't want Dad to know she'd spent fifty dollars on her daughter's temporary hair color for a costume party, so she told the girl to tell Dad it only cost twenty dollars. This is disgusting and deplorable!

Telling our children to say things like "Daddy isn't home" when you are in the next room, or "Mommy bought that at Walmart" when it really came from Nordstrom's or some other high-end store is a big fat lesson in teaching your children how to lie.

How to tell the Truth

Telling the truth isn't always easy because the essence of the human being is evil at its core but it is always necessary and always the best option. I'll agree that there are times when you shouldn't offer the truth unless you are asked (remember the outfit question), but lying is never an option you should choose if you value the person you are talking to. I have a belief that if someone lies to me then they have no respect for me, and if they have no respect for me there is nothing to build upon in any type of relationship.

It is perfectly okay to tell your children you don't know, that what they've asked is none of their business, or to say you don't want to talk about something. It is also okay to tell the truth even when the truth is not going to be popular, well-received, or accepted. You just need to make sure you do it with Christ-like grace and that your motives are pure. One of the things that I tend to do (though not necessary) is to explain my thought process to my daughter so she understands my reasoning, logic, and decision in a fuller way. This is one of the best ways to help teach your child directly how to make informed and educated decisions as they continue to grow and mature.

Now granted, there are times in which I don't do this, any parent can tell you there is a time and a place for everything, but when you have the opportunity, discuss things with your child, help them to grow in their understanding, and mature into an honorable adult that you can be proud of. Yep, that's how you make awesome kids – well at least that's one of the foundations.

Truth…it really does set you free.

Chapter 2: Health

When your children are born we experience that instant euphoria of overwhelming love for the new life we're holding, but in all that euphoria we're also doing something else. We're counting all their little fingers and toes, watching them breathe in and out, taking in the sound of those healthy cries that are signaling clear lungs and keen awareness, and then we hand them over to the one who will weigh, measure, and do all sorts of other things to pronounce them perfect and healthy.

But it doesn't stop there. We marvel at how well they can hold their head up on their own, get excited when they roll over on their own, and spread the news all over social media when they get a tooth, crawl, walk, and so on and so on. In other words, we take delight in the health and well-being of our children…as we should!

When it comes to keeping your children healthy, the best way to do that is to work from the inside out.

You can do that by making sure your children…

- Getting enough sleep. Toddlers and preschoolers need an average of 10 to 12 hours of sleep a day (including naps). Elementary age children need 8-10 hours. It is also important to keep bedtime routines consistent, to make sure they have clean air to breathe, and that they are dressed appropriately for the room temperature and how well they stay covered (or not).

- A healthy diet. Children need a healthy diet of protein, fresh fruits and veggie, carbs, whole grains and good fats from dairy and nuts. In other words, it's all about balance. I know this is hard for parents of picky eaters, so don't panic and don't force-feed them. Just make sure you offer healthy options first and that you don't cave in to giving junk food 'just so they'll have something in their stomach'. Of course they're going to choose potato chips over carrots (most of the time, anyway), so don't make chips an option.

A Great example is always to lead by example – be the example to your children, they pick up more things than you actually know and learn directly from you. So if you eat right they will be right. However, don't be a hypocrite and tell your children to eat right while you're filling your face with chips, cupcakes, and pie – this is the same thing as lying to your child.

- Eating clean. This goes along with a healthy diet, but deserves a little extra attention due to the fact that research clearly indicates that eating a diet high in processed foods, dyes, chemicals, and fake fats is directly linked to obesity, heart problems, anxiety, and behavioral problems such as ADHD, ADD, and possibly even the rise in autism.

- Get moving and take your kids with you! Children shouldn't be allowed to have more than thirty minutes to two hours in front of any kind of screen (television, computer, phone) a day depending on their age.

- This time can be in addition to school projects that require your children to be online, but try to limit school time spent in front of a screen as well. Instead, get them outside for plenty of fresh air and sunshine and good old-fashioned playtime. No real structure…just playing for the sake of playing. A swing set, jump rope, balls, a bicycle, a sandbox, and other toys that promote exercise, coordination, and using their imagination should all be a part of your child's life. Even if it's cold outside you can bundle them up for thirty or forty minutes of fresh air. Don't leave all the playing to your children, though. Play with them.

Take walks, ride bikes together, go fishing, swimming, skating…whatever your family finds enjoyable. Just keep moving

- Hand washing before eating, after using the restroom and in public places (parks, grocery store, etc.) is an important aspect of staying healthy. Don't worry about having anti-bacterial soap, though. Research is finally showing what I've thought all along—plain old soap and water is just as effective and is actually better for you. Why, you ask? Keep reading…

- Don't be a germ-a-phobe. Let your kids get dirty. A little dirt never hurt anyone. In fact, there is actually such a thing as being too clean. Yep, you heard right. Research shows that the ingredients in antibacterial soaps can mess with our body's endocrine system (hormones). Antibacterial soaps also kill good bacteria and make reduce our body's ability to fight off other forms of bad bacteria.

- Teach your children that sharing should be reserved for toys and cookies (not the same one, though).

Make sure they know that sharing the *same* food item, straws, cups, eating utensils, hair brushes and hair accessories, and hats is not wise. Colds, the flu, and head lice are passed by sharing these things.

- Prevention is worth a lot when it comes to keeping your children healthy. A healthy diet and exercise fits in here—right along with practicing good hygiene, and dressing appropriately for the weather.

- Take your children for their annual physical. Having a yearly health and wellness assessment has enabled doctors to detect problems in children before they progress to a more serious state. Along this same line is the issue of immunizations...

- More and more parents are choosing not to immunize their children. They are basing their decision on several things including:

  - The major pharmaceutical companies, Big Pharma as their known, are exempt from any prosecutions, claims, or lawsuits by anyone who takes their vaccination.

- You have to understand that the FDA has the ultimate authority over drugs in the United States and as such the United States Supreme Court in a 5 to 4 decision in the 2004 case of Karen Bartlett vs. Mutual Pharmaceutical Company ruled that if the FDA deemed the pharmaceuticals safe than they were in fact safe regardless of any adverse reactions. In fact 80% of all pharmaceuticals are exempt from any legal liability.

o   This includes immunizations
    as well as routine medication
    that millions of people use on
    a daily basis. There is no
    conspiracy here that
    immunizations cause adverse
    reactions, side effects, or
    even death – all one has to do
    is look at the federally
    mandated warning labels that
    come with all prescription
    drugs.

o Did you know that the number one cause of preventable or accidental death in the United States of America comes directly from pharmaceutical drugs, including immunizations. People who support immunizations such as the flu shot either don't know the facts who are willfully promoting immunizations for whatever purpose.

Keep in mind Big Pharma is called Big Pharma for a reason, the amount of money that these pharmaceutical companies make on a yearly basis is astronomical -so do you think they have a vested interest in getting you healthy or keeping you sick?

o   The fact that many immunizations are live-viruses should send warning flags to any decent parent out there with half a brain. Don't subject your children to these types of things.

- Research links immunizations to other health concerns including behavioral disorders and even death. The HPV Gardasil immunization for girls is once such "vaccine" that has cause numerous adverse reactions including over 30 deaths in the US alone according to the CDC. To be a great parent don't take the chance with vaccines and immunizations – the cost is just too high.

- The conviction that immunizations simply don't work. For example, scores of children (and adults) who receive the flu shot still get the flu. Another example of this is the nasal mist for the flu vaccine. It has now been deemed unsafe and ineffective after several years of being presented as a safe, effective, and viable alternative to the inoculation.

- Some parents view immunizations as a form of over-medicating, which is another problem we need to be mindful of...

- It's no secret that the general population has overmedicated themselves and their children for the last few decades. We've done so to the point of making our bodies resistant to many formerly-effective antibiotics necessary to heal our bodies from a number of illnesses. Our bodies are equipped with the means to heal themselves (to an extent). So rather than rush to the doctor at the sign of the first sniffle, give it 2-3 days (unless it gets drastically worse) before intervening with medicine.

- Another great option that many parents utilize is what's known as the holistic approach or natural healing techniques to say it in a different way. The holistic approach addresses not only the physical sickness but also addresses the psychological aspects to healing as well as the spiritual dimensions of healing that few doctors can honestly say they understand. As human beings we are not one-dimensional creatures, were not two-dimensional creatures, we live and exist in the physical, and the spiritual, and the eternal all simultaneously and in harmony with one another.

If this approach appeals to you I would encourage you to seek out a professional in your local community if there is one.

Healthy, happy children make for healthy, happy parents because when our children are healthy and happy, things are just as we want them to be – Awesome!

Chapter 3: Safety

One could easily say that the word safety is synonymous with the word love when parents are talking about their children. Keeping our children safe is one of our top priorities. From the day they take their first breath we are consumed with making sure they don't get sick or hurt and that we do whatever we can to prevent these things from happening.

In the early stages of their life we know we are solely responsible for their safety. It's up to us to make sure they are dressed warmly, that they don't get too much sun, that they get enough to eat and don't choke by taking too big a bite.

We make sure they have a safe crib to sleep in, aren't given toys that pose a danger of choking or strangulation, and we wouldn't think of leaving them unattended in the bathtub or putting them in the stroller without strapping them in. And we don't let them out of our sight when we're out in public.

When they begin to crawl and walk, we start transferring part of that responsibility over to our children.

We warn them when something is hot or sharp or a 'no-no' in order to teach them how to keep themselves safe. From there we teach them about looking both ways before crossing the street, not running through a parking lot, riding correctly in a grocery cart, not jumping from the top of the stairs or sliding down the laundry chute, and the big one…stranger-danger.

By the time our children are teenagers we have moved on to talking about cyber-bullying and cyber-predators.

We've talked to them about the dangers of drinking, drinking and driving, getting into the car with someone who has been drinking, drugs, boys who are only after one thing, and how to be aware of your surroundings in an effort to survive a school shooting, shooting in the mall or at a restaurant they work at on the weekends.

Wow! That's a lot of ground to cover and you're probably out of breath by the time you get it all said. That's okay, though, because our children need to know these things. But hearing you say them isn't enough. As a parent you need to be acting on their behalf when it comes to keeping your children safe.

There are a number of things parents need to know when it comes to keeping their children safe. As we look at the 'biggies', ask yourself if you are doing these things. If so, great! If not, read on and then get to work.

First-aid

Basic first-aid for scrapes and cuts is just that...basic. And trust me when I say you're going to get plenty of practice in administering basic first-aid when you have children around. Cleaning the cut or scrape with mild soap and water to remove dirt and debris is often all that is necessary.

Once the bleeding has stopped (if there is any) applying a thin layer of antibiotic ointment is a good idea. And the Band-Aid…the all-powerful Band-Aid (in the mind of a child) can then be applied.

Insect bites and stings are something that needs a bit more attention. Diseases carried by insect bites are real and can happen to you or your child. When your child receives a bite form an insect, you should apply ice and/or anti-itch cream (follow directions regarding infants and small children) and keep an eye on the bite to make sure it doesn't become infected.

Signs of infection include a bite that is red
and warm to touch or a bite that weeps or
has puss or a discharge. If this happens, take
your child to the doctor.

Insect stings should be handled in much the
same way as bites after you remove the
stinger with your fingers or tweezers and
apply ice or a paste of baking soda and
water or water and meat tenderizer to soothe
the pain. You can also give your child
acetaminophen to help with swelling and
pain.

Children should also be observed for allergic reactions to insect stings. The most common serious reaction is anaphylactic shock. This is a condition in which the airways swell—cutting off air supply and making it difficult or impossible to breathe. Hives, excessive swelling, and difficulty breathing are all signs of anaphylactic shock and should be given immediate attention by taking your child to the emergency room. You can also slow the effects of the allergic reaction by administering Benadryl® and/or keeping the patient cool.

NOTE: If your child has an allergic reaction to bites and stings, it is best to have an epi-pen on hand. These can be prescribed by your pediatrician.

Burns are categorized into 1st, 2nd and 3rd degree burns. First degree burns leave the skin red, warm and painful to touch but no blistering is present. This type of burn should be treated by allowing a soft stream of cool (not cold) water to run on the area for several minutes, patting it dry and covering it with a sterile bandage. No butter, ointments are necessary. OTC pain relievers can be given also if necessary.

Second degree burns are burns that include blistering, swelling, intense redness and pain. You can treat small second degree burns that the same way you treat a first degree burn. Larger second degree burns should be treated in the same way you would treat a third degree burn.

Third degree burns are burns that burn through all layers of the skin and cause permanent tissue damage. The skin may even be charred black or appear dry and white. To treat burns of this severity, you should cover the burned area with a clean, cool, moist cloth, elevate the burned area, check for breathing difficulties and seek immediate medical attention. Do NOT remove burned clothing, pour water over the burn or submerge the burn in water or attempt to remove burned skin or pop blisters.

Choking is one of a parent's greatest fears. If their child chokes will they (the parent) have the capability and mindset to act quickly and appropriately? The answer should be and can be 'yes' if you familiarize yourself with the proper procedures. As a parent it is essential for you to know the proper way to administer what is commonly known as the "Heimlich Maneuver" for infants, children, and adults.

Broken bones should be treated by seeking immediate medical attention. Broken bones need to be treated and set by a medical professional.

However, the initial treatment will likely be yours to start since you'll likely be the one present when these injuries occur. If your child suffers a broken bone, you need to immobilize the injured limb and apply ice (gently) to reduce rapid swelling and to help numb the pain. NOTE: If the fracture has caused the bone to break through the skin, stopping the bleeding should be the first course of action. Also...do not remove clothing from the injured child unless it is absolutely necessary. If it is, gently cut the fabric to get to an area of bleeding and NEVER attempt to move a child if the fracture is to any part of the body other than the legs or arms.

Parents also need to be able to perform CPR in the event your child stops breathing and to recognize the signs of and the initial treatment for a concussion and poisoning. Your pediatrician can provide you with this information as can multiple websites online.

The last thing I want to say about first-aid is simply be prepared. Make sure your home and your car are equipped with a complete first-aid kit that includes emergency numbers and basic first-aid equipment and medications. As a First Aid and CPR instructor I have taught numerous people at my job.

I have always tried to convey in a realistic way that a life hangs in the balance and your training can literally make the difference between life and death of an individual. I would highly recommend getting certified in First Aid and CPR as soon as possible. Understand having all the first-aid gear that you need is great but if you don't have the proper training it's not a balanced approach to dealing with emergency situations.

Stranger-Danger

Next on the list of safety precautions is stranger-danger. Stranger-danger is teaching your children to be cautious of strangers, to be aware of their surroundings, and to be smart when it comes to where they go, what they do, and who they are with.

The fact is you don't know if people are safe and harmless or crazy lunatics. Most people in their right mind wouldn't think of hurting a child unless they are on drugs, mentally unstable, a pedophile, or a criminal of some kind. But please understand this, there are national and global child trafficking networks that are based on satanic immersion.

Just like it only takes a tiny match to burn hundreds of thousands of acres, it only takes one deranged pervert to devastate a family by assaulting, molesting, stealing, or murdering your child. So when it comes to stranger-danger, your children needs to know the following:

- Small children should never speak to an adult stranger without your permission.
- Safe strangers will never ask them to go somewhere without your permission.
- Dangerous strangers sometimes pretend to be good people—like policemen.

Even policemen shouldn't ask a
child to go somewhere with them
without their parents' permission.

- Strangers who offer gifts and
  promises should always be reported
  – teach your kid to get away from
  them immediately and go to a "safe
  place".

To help protect your child from dangerous strangers you should do the following:

- Pray for your child's safety - Everyday.

- Give your children a 'kid code'. One parent I know gave her children a kid code—a phrase that they would need to hear an adult say before doing what the person asked them to do. In this case the kid code was "Shadrach, Meshach, and Abednego"—not something a predator is going to know.

- Tell your kids it is okay to be rude to strangers—as in ignoring them if approached or spoken to.

- Tell your kids to run and scream if approached by a stranger. Better safe than sorry if it's a false alarm.

- Don't allow your children to be unattended in the park, neighborhood, swimming pool, skating rink, movie theater, or shopping mall until you are sure they are old enough and competent enough to handle themselves appropriately in the event they are approached by a stranger.

- Talk about what your children should do and warn them of the dangers often. Do this in such a way that you make them aware and watchful, but not afraid to live life beyond the walls of your home.

- There is no one right way to do this. It depends largely on the personality of your child, so make sure you know your child in order to do this properly and effectively.

Cyber Dangers

The online world is filled with opportunities for learning, communicating, shopping, and to promote and grow business. But for all the great things the online world has to offer, there are also some bad and dangerous aspects of being so connected.

Children are especially susceptible to the dangers of the cyber world, so as their parents, that should make you especially vigilant to these potential dangers and make sure you do everything possible to keep your children cyber-safe. You can do this by:

- Requiring full and complete access to all forms of social media, online accounts, passwords, phone records, etc. IMPORTANT: This is not your ticket to being obnoxious, over-protective, embarrassing, or overly asserting yourself into your child's life. Children deserve to have conversations with their friends without your interjections and involvement.

Children are also entitled to their own opinions and thoughts without having to worry about you hounding them or criticizing them for doing so.

- Periodically check their online accounts, history, texting, etc. If nothing is illegal, dangerous, or of a nature that clearly goes against your home's principles and guidelines, don't say anything or get involved.

- If you do find something dangerous or disturbing, address the issue with your child calmly, reasonably, and with the attitude of concern for their safety and well-being. Attacking them, accusing them, and condemning them will only make the situation worse.

Create an atmosphere that discourages the possibility of cyber dangers. Block dangerous content from all tech devices in your home. Listen to uplifting music. Watch wholesome movies and television shows. Dress modestly and require your children to do the same.

- Fill your home with words from the Bible—plaques, encouraging notes to family members, refrigerator magnets, family devotions, etc..

- Pray for your children's safety and discernment.

The older and more independent our children become the more responsible they have for their own safety. As a parent you need to be ready to expect and enforce safety rules that include:

- Safe driving habits. It is best to not allow your young drivers to have passengers in their car if they are going to be driving on a roadway that allows speeds greater than 45 mph. Rules about no cell phone use should be strictly enforced, and yes, there are ways to do so. To learn what they are, check with your local law enforcement and insurance agents.

- Remind your children that you are always a phone call away and to never be afraid to call if they find themselves in an unsafe situation—even if that situation is the result of their disobedience.

- Teach your children to be aware of their surroundings. Teach them to watch for people acting suspiciously (dressed in heavy clothing when it is hot, carrying a suitcase in a mall, a teenager in an elementary school…). Teach them to be listen and pay attention to people who make threats—even if they don't seem sincere or real.

- Teach your children to remain calm in emergency situations, how to 'take cover' and how to observe from a safe distance or place.
- Make sure your children know how to defend themselves (martial arts, screaming, etc.).
- Teach and enforce rules in regards to safety in numbers, unsafe places to go, etc.

In many ways the world is a scary place. But in others it is a truly wonderful, amazing world given to us by God to enjoy. By teaching your children the how's and why's of safety, they will be able to defend themselves against the evil of the day and enjoy the amazing world we live in.

Chapter 4: Awareness

There is a fine-line that runs between being socially adept and socially awkward that is difficult to navigate no doubt—especially when things like, a scar, a learning disability, or family dynamics continually try to knock you down. Of course we're not even getting into the political correctness issue or going into a society that is hypersensitive to every little word – we'll get into that in a few.

Simply put, social skills are essential life-skills. And as a parent it is essential that you teach your children how to be socially adept among their peers, in the presence of older adults, in a crowd, in small groups, in team settings, and in situations where they're on their own. It doesn't matter whether they are homeschooled or go to private school, shy or outgoing, rick or poor, athletic or intellectual, they need to know what it means to be socially adept.

At this point I'm going to declare myself guilty of being repetitive because I'm going to repeat what I said to you in the previous chapter on teaching your children to be children and adults of Godly character and faith: Live your beliefs.

The 'do as I say-not what I do' philosophy doesn't cut it. Children really do learn what they live so you'd better be ready, willing, and able to practice what you preach at home and in public. That's right—these same reminders (call them words of warning if you'd like) are just as appropriate and necessary when it comes to teaching social skills as they are for teaching children to be Godly and faithful.

When it comes to being socially adept, the first and most important step parents need to take is to teach your children good manners and proper etiquette.

Good manners include using words like please and thank-you, excuse me, please pass the…, may I, and I'm sorry. These words are simple yet powerful and tell a great deal about a person's character.

Proper etiquette includes things like:

- Opening the door for girls/women
- Asking before borrowing something that belongs to someone else
- Not interrupting
- Waiting your turn
- Sending thank-you notes
- Saying yes mam and no sir instead of yah, and nope

- Making eye contact
- Being a good loser
- Arriving on time
- Using your inside voice when inside
- Treating yourself and others with respect

As a child I was semi-forced to take martial arts lessons. Among other things that means I heard the words 'practice makes perfect' more times than I care to remember. These words aren't only for martial art lessons, though. 'Practice makes perfect' applies to social skills, too. Yet what I have come to learn is, "Perfect Practice Leads to Perfection".

To give your children the "Perfect Practice Leads to Perfection" experiences to allow them to practice and perfect their social skills, you need to:

- Allow your children to participate in team or group activities. The activities your children participate in should be something they enjoy doing or have an interest in learning. Be careful to not over-involve your children or force them to do something they aren't comfortable with. Remember...extra-curricular activities are meant to be fun and educating.

- Expose your children to different age groups of people. Church is a great place for this to happen, but you can also take them to visit and volunteer at nursing home or retirement center and even a daycare (when they are older).

- Socialize your children among your peers, but limit so called "socialization with their peers" in their age bracket. Remember you should be the primary example to your kids. Socialization by immersion with peers of their own age is one of the greatest misconceptions in modern day parenting.

Use dinner parties that include children, game nights with two or three other families, Mom/daughter or Father/son trips as well as Mother/son and Father/daughter outings are all Excellent ways to teach your children how to interact with others in social settings.

In addition to that, you are also creating deeper bonds, making lifetime memories, and setting an example of what Godly husband-wife, parent-child, and family relationships are meant to be.

- Expose your children to different cultures by teaching them some of the norms of each culture or country.

- Practice manners and etiquette at home. Manners always matter and never go out of style. Manners and etiquette are as important to use with family as with friends and strangers.

- Give your children opportunities to use good manners and etiquette on their own (without your prompting) by allowing them to attend birthday parties, play-dates, celebrations with family friends, and to belong to children's organizations such as 4-H.

- Tailor your child's experiences when they are young to fit their personality. For example, if your child is shy and quiet, don't expect them to excel in the social graces on a little league team. That experience will be too overwhelming to them (unless they ask to play).

  Instead, your best bet would be to opt for swimming, pottery, golf, or something else that is not especially competitive.

- Be aware and in-the-know about what's going on with your child's friends and activities. Keep your eyes and ears open for signs that they are being bullied, rejected, and/or coerced into doing things they know they shouldn't for the sake of fitting in.
- Teach by example. There it is again—that reminder to be the kind of person you want your children to be.

I have a phrase I live by, not sure where I first heard it but it is this, "Lead by Example – Follow by Choice". This is the philosophy you should instill within your child regardless of their personality.

Teaching…expecting…providing opportunity. That pretty much sums it up except for one thing…you need to be willing to face the fact that there may be times when your child is the one who is not walking in integrity or doing the right thing and leading others to follow in the same types of behavior.

You know who I'm talking about…the kids who get picked last for kickball or any other kind of ball, those that don't have the 'right' shoes or clothes, the ones whose dad is doing three to five, the boy who, for reasons no one takes the time to know or understand, seems to live in his own little world of make-believe, the pregnant sixteen year old in your child's English class….these kids desperately want to fit in to…be chosen first…and smiled at…. They also deserve to be chosen, smiled at, and talked to, not talked about.

Someone's children are the ones making these kids feel this way and as difficult as it is to think about, your child could be one of them. This means your eyes and ears have to do double-duty. Not only do you need to be looking and listening for signs that your child is being bullied, labeled, etc., you need to be looking and listening for signs that your child isn't the one doing these things.

If you see the signs that your child is being a bully, you need to swallow your pride, talk to your child, and do what needs to be done to correct the situation.

You need to be concerned about your child being a bully if you notice any of the following:

- They talk about a particular child or group of children negatively by calling them names like dumb or stupid or losers or use words like 'waste of space' to describe them.
- They make racist remarks and/or refuse to interact with people who are different from them – It's not about race, It's about being part of the family of God.
- They mistreat animals or toys (theirs or those belonging to someone else).
- They are overly concerned about being popular.

They act aggressively toward others—especially those who are younger or smaller.

- They insist on wearing certain clothes, a hairstyle, or something that sets them apart from the crowd but makes them identify with part of a clique or gang.

If you notice any of these things happening in your child's life, you need to address the situation immediately. Don't hide your head in the sand and don't pass it off as just a phase.

At the same time, however, don't over-react. For example, a first-grader who calls a boy Clumsy Caleb because he dropped the ball or a third-grade girl who says boys are yucky and stupid aren't necessarily bullies with a guaranteed rap sheet in their future. They are children who need you to guide them down the path of social graces and human kindness.

Children are just that—children. They say whatever comes to mind without thinking about how it will make someone feel or affect them. But as an adult and parent, you need to be ready to step in and correct them with gentle firmness.

And by gentle firmness, I mean your correction should be a double-edged sword. One edge of the sword should convey the truth that calling people names or doing whatever bully-like act they did is wrong and mean. The other edge of the sword should send that message by Leading by Example with the right kind of behavior.

For example… Junior comes home from school laughing about the new kid who dropped his lunch tray when he tripped on his shoelace; sending food flying all over the cafeteria.

You ask if anyone helped him, to which Junior replies, "No, we were all too busy laughing." You then tell Junior how sad it makes you to know that he chose to laugh at someone in need of a friend instead of helping them out. You remind him of something he did that was embarrassing to him and you remind him of how he felt when others either laughed at him, ignored him, or helped him (whatever the case). You can also share a similar incident in your life, too.

You then end the conversation by telling Junior you are going to be praying for the new kid and for him (Junior); praying that Junior will be the kind of person Jesus wants us to be and that the new kid will have a chance to show his new peers just what type of person he really is.

What you don't do is this:

- Laugh with your child. Please tell me I don't need to explain this one!
- Tell your child you hope he drops his lunch tray and gets laughed at so he'll know just what it feels like.
- Yell at your child for being so mean and inconsiderate.

- Tell your child not to worry about it—things will work out.
- Threaten your child with punishment if they don't get their act together.
- Tell your child you are ashamed of them and their behavior.

Treating the incident by doing any of the above 'don't does' will only add fuel to the fire. Bad behavior doesn't begin overnight. It's something that happens over time as a result many things, being abused or neglected, or watching a bully in action on a continual basis.

Raising children who are socially adept happens best when you yourself are socially adept. So use your manners, practice good etiquette and be conscious of your social aptitude in order to be able to pass these qualities on to your children in such a way that they will be children and adults who are kind, gracious, respectful, respectable, and an all-around Awesome Kid.

We discussed a lot about bullying, socialization, and being adept to societal norms and expectations, however, it's important to understand that though society may change the Word of God does not. God has the same expectations now for us as he did 2000 years ago.

And though we want to be aware of societal expectations and norms it is critical not to allow these expectations and norms to fully guide you as you raise your kids. Remember God desires us to be in the world but not of the world.

The current dynamics within our society have pushed communication to the extreme. To the point where it is not uncommon to hear one another as we talk but seldom do we listen to the actual words and process them accordingly so we can actually have a conversation.

Communication is a two way street – sending and receiving information at its most simplest of forms. Political correctness, hypersensitivity and multiculturalism are cancers to our society that are destroying the very foundation of everything that this nation once stood for – Including Biblical Principles.

In fact, in today's modern American society it's not uncommon, especially on liberal college campuses to find those that have been offended or traumatized merely by words that are commonly used.

Again, regardless of the society that you live in it's important to teach your children how to stand fast and proclaim what they truly believe regardless of if it offends someone or not. I do my best to teach my daughter three core pillars, "Faith, Family, and Freedom". Since we're talking about what I teach my daughter it's also important to understand that with issues like bullying they can be easily avoided by homeschooling. There are so many different bullying campaigns going on throughout the nation but if you look a little deeper you'll see that the majority of issues pertaining to bullying stem from government run schools.

Private schools have a dramatically lower rate of issues pertaining to bullying and as I mentioned with homeschooling you can pretty much eliminate any such issues. However, will get to education in just a minute.

Chapter 5: Education

You'd be hard-pressed to find a parent anywhere in the world who isn't in favor of giving their children every possible opportunity to get a quality education. An education is one of those things that is never a waste of time. The question many parents have, however, is the question of what constitutes a quality education.

Parents basically have three options for providing a quality education for our children: homeschooling, private schools, or the government school system.

There is a *definite* right or wrong answer on which choice you make for your children's education – but this is your choice. For some families in different situations a government or private school education is the best option, but for others, homeschooling is the only way to go.

The decision is a very personal one and one every family should be able to make without being made to feel guilty about or being disrespected or ridiculed for. So in order to be both respectful and fair, I will present the information to you as best I can in the most professional way I can.

Some people hate homeschool, some people hate government schools -both sides of the 'fence' have their own views and points but you have to do what's best for you and your family. Let's take a few minutes to take a look at some of the *possible* pros and cons of each of the three options for educating your children.

NOTE: I will not be labeling the possible pros and cons as such—that's for YOU to decide for YOUR family and situation

.

Homeschooling

Homeschooling is the term used to define parent-administered education. Homeschooling is essentially just what the name implies—'going' to school at home. While homeschooling has been gaining tremendous popularity over the last twenty years or so, it certainly isn't a new concept. Homeschooling has been around for centuries. Think about it…what other option did mothers have for teaching their children to read, write, and 'cipher' while traveling across the country on a wagon train or living in remote areas once they arrived at their destination?

Likewise, the children living in small communities that couldn't attract or afford to pay a teacher did also depended on homeschooling to give their children the most basic skills. However, they learned whenever they could fit it in between everything else they needed to do to survive. Missionaries living all over the world have been homeschooling their children for decades out of necessity and a desire to provide their children with an education that is more in-depth than what is available in government run schools.

Abraham Lincoln, Albert Einstein, C.S. Lewis, Booker T. Washington, Woodrow Wilson, Thomas Jefferson, and more recently, Venus and Serena Williams were all homeschooled.

The resurgence of popularity in homeschooling started approximately thirty years ago. The reasons most frequently cited for doing so at the time were faith-based. Parents did not want their children being taught that things like evolution, sex, and abortion were acceptable and right, while being ridiculed and slammed for believing otherwise.

Today, however, the choice to homeschool is made based on a much broader and extensive set of reasons that range from faith and religious values to being able to better serve the special needs of their children, safety issues, and the ability to offer a more quality curriculum than most government schools can offer.

Today there are over 2.3 million children in the United States learning in a homeschool setting. These children represent all races, socio-economic backgrounds, religions, and geographical demographics. In other words, homeschooling is a viable option for every family if they want it to be.

So what does homeschooling offer you and your child?

- Costs less than government or private schools. According to the National Home Education Research Institute, the average family spends $600 a year per child for a homeschool education vs. $5,000 for the average private school tuition, plus uniforms and $800 for government school lunches and misc. fees. NOTE: The amount spent on school supplies and clothing were not considered since these expenses will be incurred no matter what option of education you choose for your children.

The amount of money the school spends on each child per year is also not included, as that is primarily tax-payer funded and everyone paying taxes contributes to that.

- Gives children the capability of learning at their own speed and allows learning to be tailored to their specific learning style.

- Allows for the use of online coursework through colleges and universities geared specifically for the homeschool setting, OER (Open Educational Resources), and the option of classes not always available in government or private schools.

- Gives parents more oversight as to what is being taught.
- Offers greater flexibility for families, especially if they are RVing full time
- Offers greater opportunity for parental choice for socially appropriate interactions
- Provides parents with a greater degree of control and choice over their child's socialization and peer-interaction.
- Allows parents to present life-views and moral values freely and openly.
- Provides for a safer environment in the way of bullying, violence, and exposure to lifestyles and views before children are emotionally and spiritually equipped to handle them.

- Makes parents responsible for being diligent, organized, and for making their child's education a priority in their day to day life.

- Allows for bonding: parents and children to spend the majority of their time together.

- Allows parents and children to seek out opportunities for extra-curricular activities that will allow them to grow and mature socially, emotionally, and to hone their talents and abilities.

- Requires a great deal of self-discipline for everyone involved.

- Requires a great deal of planning, organization, and commitment to follow through to ensure children are progressing as they should.
- Allows for flexibility for family outings, vacations, emergencies, and family circumstances such as relocating, etc.

Government school

Government schools used to be the assumed norm. Everyone except the Catholic kids went to public school. And that was fine because parents assumed that when they sent their kids to school they would be safe. They would learn from teachers who were there to teach.

Yes, some of them were much nicer and more fun than others, but they all were there because they wanted to teach us something. Children were also disciplined and for the most part, values like respect for God and country and for others was taught and expected to be the norm – Well at least in the 1950's.

Today...not so much. Today government schools are being mandated by people who are so far removed from the students and teachers themselves that they don't have any idea of what really needs to be done.

What's more, because government schools are tax-funded, they are strongly state-church-separation oriented. Does anyone remember what happened to our country when they took prayer out of our government run schools?

This isn't to say all government schools are bad and that sending your child to government schools makes you a bad parent. Not at all! The fact of the matter is that for many families government schools are your only option. Think about it...how are single-parent families going to work all day and homeschool their children?

The key to successful government schooling lies in being vigilant and involved in your child's government run school education. Yet this vigilance and involvement may equal that same amount of time that it would take to homeschool your child. Your community also plays a huge role in the quality of your government funded school system – normally the ethics, morals, and values of the local community will be reflected in your local government school regardless of federal mandates and politics.

Government schools…

- Allows the State to Educate YOUR Child in the Way they Feel is Right
- Do put your child at serious risk from bullying, violence, gangs, politics and a host of other concerns including teachers who are petrifies, registered sex offenders, or those into child pornography. Understand these people always try to get close to their victims.
- Teaches Obedience by providing an organized and structured education.
- Ensure teaching is done by those with State Licenses

- Provides students with opportunities to socialize and interact with their peers on a daily basis and learn directly from them.
- Requires children to be accepting of those different from them, including embracing different faith and doctrines.
- Offers opportunities for extra-curricular activities
- Offer free services for learning disabilities, tutoring, and health services not otherwise available.
- Cannot and will not openly promote Christian values.

- Are often unable to teach due to increasing disciplinary issues they are forced to deal with.
- Can offer scholarship opportunities to students not otherwise available or accessible.

Private school

Private schools are considered by some to be the homeschool for working parents. Private schools offer a more structured, controlled environment than public schools while providing students the opportunity to interact with peers who usually have similar beliefs and lifestyles.

This statement isn't meant to be judgmental or discriminatory. But the fact that the majority of private schools are operated by churches, specifically for gifted or special-needs students, or are traditionally comprised of students from wealthy families makes it a true statement. Not bad. Just true.

Private schools:

- Are expensive and usually have a waiting list.
- Often attract high caliber teachers.
- Provide a greater sense of security and safety but still face teachers abusing their positions to take advantage of students at times.

- Usually have the newest and best in facilities, materials, and resources.
- Usually holds students to a higher degree of responsibility, respect, and performance.
- Are smaller than most public schools so the teacher to student ratio is more student-friendly.
- Usually require uniforms; reducing the problematic issue of discrimination and negative peer pressure.
- Can provide specialized education for children with special needs or those who are gifted that is far more adequate than homeschooling or public schools can provide.

- Are respected by colleges and universities
- Have less accountability then government run schools.

The choice should be made Jointly

To homeschool or not...that is a decision for both parents to make together. It is one that should be based on both yours and your child's personality, your ability to stay on task and to be organized and thorough. Remember...your child's education is something you should both take very seriously. Your child's personality in regards to whether they are easily persuaded or not should also be taken into consideration as well as their age.

Your child should also have some small degree of input into which option you choose – just remember they are a child and you have the responsibility to make the best decision as a parent. Some children prefer to be homeschooled while others crave the social interaction they experience while learning among their peers. Again you are the parent – do what you feel is right.

Some families see homeschooling as the best way to ensure their children grow up with the values, morals, and religious convictions they need in order to go out into the world as young adults.

I must say that families feel that by sending
their children to government or private
schools are teaching their children to be salt
and light to a world in need of Jesus is a
very twisted concept of that idea. You don't
send a vulnerable child that is not fully
developed in their mind, body, spirit, or soul
into what I consider to be a war zone and tell
them to preach the Word. That concept is
non-sense – Look at any Military or Army –
You don't see kids in uniforms holding
weapons do you. The same should be true of
our kids don't send them to the battle field
until they are older and ready to stand and
fight.

I know, I know I was trying to be impartial
but the reality is I am partial and believe that
Homeschooling is the Absolute best option
if you are able to do it. If you need help
getting started and you live in Maryland
contact us though our website at
www.acdainc.org. We do have a
Homeschool Umbrella that we offer to those
in our organization.

The bottom line is this, when all is said and
done the choice for educating your children
should come down to what will work best
for your family while at the same time allow
you to fulfill your obligation to your
children to raise them up to know and love
the Lord.

Chapter 6: Boys and Girls

This is going to be the shortest chapter of this book—not because it isn't important, but because God has spoken clearly and plainly on the subject of gender, sexuality, and what constitutes a marriage and family. So rather than filling pages with words that are mine, I'm simply going to tell you what God, who happens to be the ultimate authority on the matter, has to say and leave it at that. Well, almost at that...

The following verses are taken from the King James Version of the Bible. All verses are in italics and my thoughts are in regular print.

"So God created man in his own image, in the image of God created he him; male and female created he them." ~ KJV

"For every creature of God is good, and nothing to be refused, if it be received with thanksgiving: For it is sanctified by the word of God and prayer." ~1ˢᵗ Timothy 4:4-5 KJV

A friend of mine who has spent nearly thirty years in youth ministry and raised four children of her own is 'famous' for regularly reminding her children (biological and otherwise) that "God don't make no junk!"

She's right. God doesn't make junk or mistakes, so for someone to claim they were born the wrong sex is a lie. It is blasphemy. God created us perfectly and for specific reasons.

"For God is not the author of confusion, but of peace, as in all churches of the saints".
~1 Corinthians 14:33 KJV

Did you get that? God isn't the author of confusion. This means when He created us He didn't create us with the possibility of being confused about our sexuality.

"If a man also lie with mankind, as he lieth with a woman, both of them have committed an abomination: they shall surely be put to death; their blood shall be upon them"
~Leviticus 20:13 KJV

And likewise also the men, leaving the natural use of the woman, burned in their lust one toward another; men with men working that which is unseemly, and receiving in themselves that recompence of their error which was meet. ~Romans 1:27 KJV

These two passages of scripture clearly and plainly state that homosexuality is a sin. This truth also means that "same-sex marriages" are sinful.

"And he answered and said unto them, Have ye not read, that he which made them at the beginning made them male and female ... "
~Matthew 19:4 KJV

This verse, along with the one being referenced here (Genesis 1:27) tells us we are made in the image of God. Because this is true, to be transgender, homosexual, or bi-sexual is in complete opposition to God's original creation of us and against His will.

Once more, when someone submits themselves to living a lifestyle that embraces or even accepts these sins as okay, they are separating themselves from God just as they do when they submit themselves to any other sin.

Nevertheless neither is the man without the woman, neither the woman without the man, in the Lord"~1 Corinthians 11:11 KJV

"Know ye not that the unrighteous shall not inherit the kingdom of God? Be not deceived: neither fornicators, nor idolaters, nor adulterers, nor effeminate, nor abusers of themselves with mankind, nor thieves, nor covetous, nor drunkards, nor revilers, nor extortioners, shall inherit the kingdom of God" ~1 Corinthians 6:9-10 KJV

"The woman shall not wear that which pertaineth unto a man, neither shall a man put on a woman's garment: for all that do so are abomination unto the LORD thy God" ~Deuteronomy 22:5 KJV

Talking to your children about sexuality and gender identification

Now more than ever, parents need to step up to the plate when it comes to teaching your children right from wrong about gender identification and sexuality. And when I say right from wrong, I mean God's views vs. the world's views.

As a parent you need to make sure our children know and understand what the Bible has to say on the subject. But you also need to make sure your children know and understand that sexual sins are no different or worse than any other sin. Sin is sin in God's eyes so it should be in ours, as well.

When you are having these conversations with your children you are undoubtedly going to be asked questions like:

- Aren't we supposed to love everyone?
- If it's so wrong then why do so many people think it's okay?
- Should we allow homosexuals or transgenders to come to church?
- How am I supposed to act around someone who is gay or transgender?
- Is it wrong to shop or do business with places who say these things are okay?
- What should I do if I go into a bathroom and someone of the opposite sex who claims to be transgender is in there?

While I can't tell you exactly what to say, the following answers or guidelines should help...

- Yes, we are supposed to love our brother and sisters in Christ but not the things of this world that God hates. Loving someone doesn't mean letting them have their way all the time or allowing them to believe they are right when they aren't.

You can follow this answer by giving examples such as this: Your love for them (your child) doesn't mean you let them do whatever they want and it certainly doesn't mean you never discipline them or tell them when they are doing something they shouldn't. In fact, it is because you love them that you correct them.

- People think all sorts of things are okay that aren't. For example, people who use drugs don't do so because they want to become addicts. Also, people who believe pre-marital sex is okay or those who think nothing of stealing, speeding, drinking underage, or using foul language are okay and acceptable doesn't make it so.

- Yes, we should most definitely 'allow' and invite homosexuals and transgenders to church. We are all sinners in need of the Savior. But just like any and every other sin, being part of the church and accepting Christ as Savior demands that you repent from your sins and sinful lifestyles. This means that coming into the church as a transgender or homosexual doesn't give someone the option or right to remain in their sin.

- You are to treat 'these people' as you would anyone else—with kindness and respect. We can be kind without being accepting of their beliefs and lifestyles. We also have the right to expect the same from them.

- Sadly in this day and age it is next to impossible to not shop or do business with people who are accepting of the world's views of sexuality and gender identification but if your convictions are strong enough you can do it. Target is a great example of how boycotting a company based on their support or endorsement of the LGBT agenda.

The decision of where to shop and who to do business with is a personal one that only you and your family can make for yourselves but just remember to Lead by Example and follow your convictions as your kids are sure to follow in your footsteps as they mature.

- Another sad situation…not being able to feel safe or comfortable when using public restrooms or even restrooms at school or on the job. The best way to handle this situation is to not allow children under the age of ten to enter a public restroom on their own.

For children over the age of ten you need to make sure they understand to leave the rest room immediately if a person of the opposite sex enters that restroom you're are in – run don't walk! If stores or the government are permitting transgenders to have the "right" to enter the restroom, understand that your kids have more of a right to feel and be safe. Instruct your children to secure the door on their booth, to make their visit as brief as possible, and to not make eye contact with the person. It is said that avoiding eye contact reduces the chances of being assaulted by someone posing as a transgender.

Your children should also know they have every right to report any situation that makes them feel unsafe to authorities (store managers, teachers, and especially, you). This is where have an open and honest relationship comes in, remember the first chapter about Never Lying to Your Kids.

You don't have to join 'Em

The world is full of evil and is changing rapidly. And can I say that the changes aren't positive. In spite of it all, we shouldn't lose sight of the fact that God is and will forever be the master of the universe and when all is said and done He will have the final say.

For those who remain faithful, obedient, and steadfast in living according to His Word, this fact is comforting, reassuring, and something worth holding on to.

Chapter 7: Spiritual Upbringing

The title for this chapter comes from the Bible—specifically Proverbs 22:6 that says, *"Train up a child in the way he should go: and when he is old, he will not depart from it".*

As parents we have a responsibility to raise our children to know the Lord. Yes, a responsibility, because our children are as I like to say, "On loan to us from God."

In speaking to other parents on the subject of raising Godly children, I remind them that, "When God entrusts us to raise His children we have the responsibility of returning them to Him some day in which they will hear the words, "Well Done Good and Faithful Servant".

Take a minute to read over that statement again and let it sink in. Do you get what I'm saying? God presented us with perfect little babies with the intention that we would raise them to know and love Him so that they have the hope of heaven when they die.

Now I know putting the words 'children' and 'death' aren't pleasant but it's something you need to keep tucked away in order to help you remain diligent, firm, and faithful in your efforts to raise your children to have a personal relationship with the Lord –and if they do, you've been a great parent and raised and Awesome Kid.

I know it's not easy with everything going on in the world today. Former President Dwight Eisenhower once said that people who value their rights and privileges more than they value their principles soon lose both. And oh, how right he was. But here's a newsflash for you:

There's always been a lot of unpleasantness and evil going on in the world, and it's never been easy to raise children to choose God over the world. If you don't believe that, think about:

- The reason God wiped out mankind with a flood (except for Noah and his family)
- Sodom and Gomorrah
- Nineveh
- Nero's rule of Rome
- The Holocaust
- Isis

It should come as no surprise that each generation thinks their young people are worse than they were. This is a pattern we've seen for decades. You know what I'm talking about. You remember hearing your grandparents say things like, "Back in my day we wouldn't have even thought about doing…." Or, "If I would have talked to my parents like that…."

But there is a reason adults have been saying these things for the past several generations. It's true. While we may think things are not as bad as Sodom and Gomorrah, statistics and headlines tell a different story.

Sexual assault, predator stalking, child trafficking, murder, and crimes that shout disrespect of people and property are on the rise and have been for quite some time. Issues like pornography, homosexuality, and premarital sex are no longer seen as sin, but as a normal part of life. Once more, church involvement and religious beliefs in young people are at an all-time low and the sense of community and living the Golden Rule are the exception rather than the rule. But like I said, all is not lost.

It is possible to raise Godly children to be Godly adults if you take the following encouragements to heart:

- Live your beliefs. The 'do as I say-not what I do' philosophy doesn't cut it. Children really do learn what they live so you'd better be ready, willing, and able to practice what you preach at home and in public.

- Openly discuss your religious beliefs with your children. Answer their questions and work towards helping your child make those beliefs their own,-not just something they say or do because you do.

When your children are small they will naturally follow your lead, but the older they get the more independent they become in their thinking. That's a good thing. It's what's supposed to happen. But you need to make sure you do your best to give them a solid foundation from the very beginning so they can independently embrace the Godly values and doctrine you want them to.

- Be polite, considerate and respectful of your children. This whole, "You-have-to-give-respect-to-Get-respect" philosophy has to start somewhere and when it comes to parenting, it needs to begin with you.

You teach your children to be honest by being honest. You teach them what a strong work-ethic looks like by having one yourself. You teach them respect by showing them what respect looks like by giving it to them.

- Monitor your child's media: music, movies, television, computer, video games, books and magazines. Don't let anyone tell you these things don't make a difference because they do! Satan is eager and active to snatch your children up and shape their opinions and thoughts by using music, movies, games, and websites.

He is equally anxious to attack their self-esteem and demoralize them by convincing them to adopt the world's standards when it comes to how they dress, talk, and act.

- Keep an open dialogue with your children—not just about the big things like faith, dating, grades, friends, and such. The more conversations you have about the everyday things in life the more conversations you'll have about the big things.

- Read, study, and discuss the Bible together as a family. Use the Bible as a foundation for the rules, expectations, and guidelines for your family.

- Provide opportunities for your children to serve others and make serving others a regular part of your family's activities. Make sure some of these service projects get them (and you) out of their comfort zone in an effort to grow compassionate, self-less hearts and minds. When you share your 'stuff', your time, talents, and money with others, your children will learn to do the same.

- Don't allow gossip, racism and arrogance to be part of your family's life.

- Be involved in the church and require your children to do the same. Okay, here's the deal…showing up on Saturday or Sunday morning to sit in a pew, sing a few songs, listen to the preacher, take communion, and toss in a few "Amen's" with your money doesn't cut it. If that made you cringe, I'm sorry. Wait, no I'm not. I'm not sorry for telling the truth and the truth is this: If you want your children to really know who Jesus is and have a personal relationship with Him, they need to be involved in the church.

They need to know their church family, be spiritually nurtured and fed both collectively and personally by serving, worshipping, learning, and fellowshipping together. However, to clarify the true Church is not a building, denomination, or set of religious pretenses – The Church is those brothers and sisters who hear the Word of God and Do it consistently. You and Your Family's Allegiance is not to your, so-called "church" that operates out of a building somewhere. Your Allegiance is to Christ and to follow His Word regardless of what your church thinks about it or the world for that matter.

I have a saying that I live by and teach my daughter, "Think For Yourself and Learn Directly From God." This philosophy sums up the essence of your duties to teach your kids how to develop Spiritually in the Christian Faith. Help instill this mindset and you will be well on your way to raising Awesome Kids.

- Pray for your children. Pray for their health. Pray for their friends. Pray for their future spouse. Pray for their safety. Pray for their teachers, if its not you. Pray for their self-esteem. Pray for their future career and business. Pray for their faith and that they will allow God to fulfill His purpose for their life.

Did you get that? Pray! Prayer is a Powerful equalizer against the forces of darkness that try to get your kids of track. The simple fact is, "Great Parents Pray for their Kids".

Your best efforts still may not be Enough

Now for the disclaimer portion of this chapter: in spite of your best efforts in living out your faith and teaching your children the value of living a godly life, some children may reject your belief system for those of others or simply create their own. The Bible makes it very clear that there are vessels for honor and dishonor.

But in a great house there are not only vessels of gold and of silver, but also of wood and of earth; and some to honour, and some to dishonour." ~ *2 Tim 2:20, KJV*

In fact Jesus himself said, "that a prophet is not without honor except in his own house" - I'm paraphrasing a bit on that last Scripture but the point is the same

"But Jesus, said unto them, A prophet is not without honour, but in his own country, and among his own kin, and in his own house." ~ *Mark 6:4, KJV*

I know, it's not easy or pleasant to think about—the fact that your own children might reject the firm and loving foundation of faith you provided them. But it happens. Sometimes their rebellion and rejection is temporary but there are also those who never return to the faith, or maybe they never truly had it.

Wait! That can't be! The Bible says if we train our children up right they won't depart from it when they are old. So what's that all about? This verse is commonly mistaken to mean that if you raise your children to know the Lord they won't turn their back on Him—or not for good if they temporarily go astray.

But this verse is not a promise or is it? Is it a guarantee? This verse isn't a "Thus sayeth the Lord" verse. It is a wise comment made by King Solomon that God deemed worthy of being included in the Bible.

The exact translation for the word 'train' in Proverbs 22:6 is the word 'chanak', which literally means to put in their mouth. The less literal translation of the word means to enter them into the proper place. So while we like to use the verse in the context of Spiritual Upbrining, the truth of the matter is that this verse isn't focusing on 'just' Godly training.

This verse is talking about raising your children to follow their natural talents and abilities and to live a life that is best-suited for who they are in general so God can use them.

Paul writes to Timothy about a similar matter in the following verse:

"And that from a child thou hast known the holy scriptures, which are able to make thee wise unto salvation through faith which is in Christ Jesus. All scripture is given by inspiration of God, and is profitable for doctrine, for reproof, for correction, for instruction in righteousness That the man of God may be perfect, thoroughly furnished unto all good works." ~ 2 Tim 3:16, KJV

The fact is that the Bible declares we should work out our own salvation with fear and trembling before the Lord.

"Wherefore, my beloved, as ye have always obeyed, not as in my presence only, but now much more in my absence, work out your own salvation with fear and trembling."
Phil. 2:12, KJV

At this point you may be thinking why bother or thanks for raining on my parade, but that's not my intention. My intention in giving you this truth in addition to the encouragements on how to raise awesome Godly children is to remind you that God gives us all free choice—and 'all' includes your children.

As parents we are to guide and lead our children as best as we possibly can in the straight and narrow way but ultimately each child grows into an adult and must make their own decision to follow God or not. Salvation is a free gift that can be accepted or rejected at any time but God in his grace and mercy has enabled you to read these words and help you raise awesome kids that love the Lord and you. So as long as you do your best to live up to your responsibility of raising your kids to know Jesus on a real and personal level, you are doing your job. Don't beat yourself up. Don't feel guilty. Don't feel like you failed. Just keep praying and doing what you can.

In fact the Bible offers great hope for parents of the faith in the story of the prodigal son found below:

And he said, A certain man had two sons:And the younger of them said to his father, Father, give me the portion of goods that falleth to me. And he divided unto them his living. And not many days after the younger son gathered all together, and took his journey into a far country, and there wasted his substance with riotous living. And when he had spent all, there arose a mighty famine in that land; and he began to be in want. And he went and joined himself to a citizen of that country; and he sent him into his fields to feed swine.

And he would fain have filled his belly with the husks that the swine did eat: and no man gave unto him. And when he came to himself, he said, How many hired servants of my father's have bread enough and to spare, and I perish with hunger! I will arise and go to my father, and will say unto him, Father, I have sinned against heaven, and before thee, And am no more worthy to be called thy son: make me as one of thy hired servants. And he arose, and came to his father. But when he was yet a great way off, his father saw him, and had compassion, and ran, and fell on his neck, and kissed him. And the son said unto him, Father, I have sinned against heaven, and in thy sight, and am no more worthy to be called thy son.

But the father said to his servants, Bring forth the best robe, and put it on him; and put a ring on his hand, and shoes on his feet: And bring hither the fatted calf, and kill it; and let us eat, and be merry: For this my son was dead, and is alive again; he was lost, and is found. And they began to be merry. Now his elder son was in the field: and as he came and drew nigh to the house, he heard music and dancing. And he called one of the servants, and asked what these things meant. And he said unto him, Thy brother is come; and thy father hath killed the fatted calf, because he hath received him safe and sound. And he was angry, and would not go in: therefore came his father out, and intreated him.

*And he answering said to his father, Lo,
these many years do I serve thee, neither
transgressed I at any time thy
commandment: and yet thou never gavest
me a kid, that I might make merry with my
friends: But as soon as this thy son was
come, which hath devoured thy living with
harlots, thou hast killed for him the fatted
calf. And he said unto him, Son, thou art
ever with me, and all that I have is thine."
~Luke 15:11-31, KJV*

~Amen!

Chapter 8:

Political Involvement

As I write this we are knee-deep in preparation for electing our next president. The rhetoric and sparring this time around are unprecedented. Never have I seen or heard so much discussion and emotion surrounding an election. You might be wondering at this point why I'm mentioning politics in a parenting book. The simple fact is if you want to be a great parent and raise awesome kids you have to teach them how to stand against evil, corruption, and the constant destruction that governments cause. Furthermore you have to teach them the appropriate amount of involvement for a Christian to have regarding politics.

Make no mistake about it, to quote Steve Quayle, "There is no Political Solution to a Spiritual Problem" But as far as I am concerned we still need to "Stand In The Gap".

Some Christians believe that as Christians we should not be involved in any form of politics while others believe we should attempt to enter in the Kingdom of God here on earth through political means. I would say that both assumptions would be incorrect. God commands us to occupy until his return – what does that mean to you?

It could be argued that Christians who don't involve themselves in any form of politics are in fact part of the problem and the mess were currently in. Edmund Burke said it best, "The only thing necessary for the triumph of evil is for good men to do nothing." Time and time again we see examples in the Word of God in which God calls us to stand fast, stand in the gap, to come against evil, or even to war against the enemies of God.

So many Christians in Modern Day American "Churches" quote Romans 13:1 to justify their full submission to whatever the governments of this world say or do – This is called the Submission doctrine and it is completely false. Rom 13:1 was the justification for Monarchies throughout the world prior to the United States Revolutionary War. Thomas Paine wrote very elegantly about the insanity of the establishment of Monarchies in his work, "Common Sense". If you haven't ever read this, I would highly suggest you do so. It was the one document that rallied the Colonies and United them in purpose. A little known fact about Hitler was that Rom 13:1 was one of his favorite verses in the Bible.

According to Rummel (the developer of the modern day term and concept of democide), democide surpassed war as the leading cause of non-natural death in the 20th century (wikipedia.org). Understand this, the number one cause of death in the world is still from democide - even today. For those that were wondering, "Democide is a term revived and redefined by the political scientist R. J. Rummel (1932–2014) as "the murder of any person or people by their government, including genocide, politicide and mass murder".(wikipedia.org).

And yet Romans 13:1 say the following:

"Let every soul be subject unto the higher powers. For there is no power but of God: the powers that be are ordained of God." ~ *Rom. 13:1*

So some immediate questions come to mind after reading Romans 13:1. Some of these questions include the following:

- If we know that the whole world is swayed by the wicked one why should we completely submit to all authority and let them rule over us since they are in fact evil?

*"And we know that we are of God,
and the whole world lieth in
wickedness."* ~ 1 John 5:19, KJV

- Why should we submit to an earthly
  government when the Kings of the
  earth plot a vain thing again the Lord
  and against His people?

*"Why do the heathen rage, and the
people imagine a vain thing? The
kings of the earth set themselves, and
the rulers take counsel together,
against the Lord, and against his
anointed, saying,*

Let us break their bands asunder,
and cast away their cords from us.
He that sitteth in the heavens shall
laugh: the Lord shall have them in
derision. Then shall he speak unto
them in his wrath, and vex them in
his sore displeasure. Yet have I set
my king upon my holy hill of Zion. I
will declare the decree: the Lord
hath said unto me, Thou art my Son;
this day have I begotten thee. Ask of
me, and I shall give thee the heathen
for thine inheritance, and the
uttermost parts of the earth for thy
possession. Thou shalt break them
with a rod of iron; thou shalt dash
them in pieces like a potter's vessel.

Be wise now therefore, O ye kings:
be instructed, ye judges of the earth.
Serve the Lord with fear, and rejoice
with trembling. Kiss the Son, lest he
be angry, and ye perish from the
way, when his wrath is kindled but a
little. Blessed are all they that put
their trust in him" ~Psalms 2, KJV

- Why should we submit when Jesus
  Himself did not? How did Jesus
  handle the question of government
  and rulers? To say that Jesus was a
  rebel would be putting it mildly.

Jesus was a nonconformist in every aspect but one, He conformed to the Word of God and to the Word of God only – for in fact He was the literal manifestation of the Word of God.

"And they brought it. And he saith unto them, Whose is this image and superscription? And they said unto him, Caesar's. And Jesus answering said unto them, Render to Caesar the things that are Caesar's, and to God the things that are God's. And they marvelled at him"

- When a government turns completely evil and the foundations of truth, justice, and law are not being honored they have thus been destroyed by default. So are we still to submit to that?

  "For, lo, the wicked bend their bow, they make ready their arrow upon the string, that they may privily shoot at the upright in heart. If the foundations be destroyed, what can the righteous do?" ~ Psalms 11:3, KJV

Yet in 1 Peter 2:13-17 we read a Scripture Verse similar to Rom 13:1

> *"Submit yourselves to every ordinance of man for the Lord's sake: whether it be to the king, as supreme; Or unto governors, as unto them that are sent by him for the punishment of evildoers, and for the praise of them that do well. For so is the will of God, that with well doing ye may put to silence the ignorance of foolish men: As free, and not using your liberty for a cloke of maliciousness, but as the servants of God. Honour all men. Love the brotherhood. Fear God. Honour the king." ~ 1 Peter 2:13-17, KJV*

So what's the bottom line here? What is the Scriptures indicating? Well regarding Romans 13 and the group of scriptures associated with that particular chapter indicating to submit to all government authority is actually talking and referring to a spiritual government not a physical government here on earth. Just think about it for a second, why would Christ want us to submit to an evil government that is under the control and the power of the wicked one – does that make any sense?

Regarding 1 Peter 2:13 – 17 this is simply referring to respecting the laws of the land, the king or government authority by walking in righteousness so that the glory of the Lord will be reflected in you as a living epistle read by all men that some may, through your conduct come to know the Lord in a real and person way. It is referring to not being a hypocrite and walking in reproach which is truly a snare of the devil.

Jesus said it best, render to Caesar the things that are Caesar's and to God the things that are God"s.

Founding Fathers of Our Nation

- It's important to understand that our nation has a long history of men and women of faith. In fact the majority of the Founding Fathers of Our Nation believed in God. They took Biblical principles together with what history had taught them about other nations and created the Declaration Of Independence and The Constitution of the United States of America.

Quotes from the Founding Fathers:

- *"It is the duty of all nations to acknowledge the providence of Almighty God, to obey His will, to be grateful for His benefits, and humbly to implore His protection and favor." – George Washington*

- *We beseech [God] to pardon our national and other transgressions... – George Washington, Thanksgiving Proclamation 1789*

- *The rights of the colonists as Christians...may be best understood by reading and carefully studying the institutes of the Great Law Giver and Head of the Christian Church, which are to be found clearly written and promulgated in the New Testament. – Samuel Adams*

- *"The Congress of the United States recommends and approves the Holy Bible for use in all schools." – United States Congress 1782*

- *The highest glory of the American Revolution was this: it connected, in one indissoluble bond, the principles of civil government with the principles of Christianity. – John Adams*

- *Our Constitution was made only for a moral and religious people. It is wholly inadequate to the government of any other. – John Adams*
- *Let the children...be carefully instructed in the principles and obligations of the Christian religion. This is the most essential part of education. – Benjamin Rush (signer of the Declaration of Independence)*

- *In my view, the Christian religion is the most important and one of the first things in which all children, under a free government ought to be instructed ... No truth is more evident to my mind than that the Christian religion must be the basis of any government intended to secure the rights and privileges of a free people. – Noah Webster, Preface Noah Webster Dictionary, 1828*

The quotes supporting the truth that our nation was meant to be a nation under God are numerous and undeniable in their message. The question is how did we get so far off course? According to the founding fathers there is an obvious answer, "We Have Lost Our Faith".

This government was constructed and structured to operate only for a moral and just people, i.e. people of faith. We can look around and blame all the politicians, the media, drugs, addictions, or pornography but the fact remains that, "As Goes the Church, As Goes America."

America is simply a reflection, a mirror if you would of the sickness that is within the church. False doctrines, secular humanism, and LGBT clergy have infiltrated the church and infected it with the disease called sin.

We've also gotten off course because the Church (meaning Christians) have allowed it to happen. We've sat back and allowed the "little things" to creep in.

You know, things like allowing children's sports leagues and coaches to play games and hold practices during church times, looking the other way when religious Christmas carols and nativity scenes were banished from schools and public property, removing prayer from our classrooms, approving of sex, cursing, and violence on television and the movies, and demoting church attendance to the status of holidays and an if-we-don't-have-anything-better-to-do activity.

The only way that we can make America Great again is by making the church great again – and only way that we make the church great again is by individually being accountable to God for the actions that we take, and the actions that we don't take, it has to start with us and by extension our kids. We have to Humble Ourselves before the Lord and Repent so that we may experience His grace, mercy, and providence once more

> "If my people, which are called by my name, shall humble themselves, and pray, and seek my face, and turn from their wicked ways; then will I hear from heaven, and will forgive their sin, and will heal their land." 2 Chorn. 7:14, KJV

"For I know the thoughts that I think toward you, saith the LORD, thoughts of peace, and not of evil, to give you an expected end. Then shall ye call upon me, and ye shall go and pray unto me, and I will hearken unto you. And ye shall seek me, and find me, when ye shall search for me with all your heart." ~ Jer. 29:11-13, KJV

Remember:

Lead by Example – Follow by Choice.

- The question parents have is how to get the job done. How do we parent our children to respect God first and government second with everything we're being faced with these days?
- First and foremost, pray! Pray for our nation. Pray for our leaders. Pray for our schools. Pray for our teachers. Pray for our law enforcement officers. Pray for the Church. Pray for your kids and your family.
- Secondly, know what the Bible says and base your thoughts, opinions, words, and actions solely on God's Word.

Don't just pick and choose, though. Living the Christian life is an all or nothing lifestyle not just something you do when it feels good, is convenient, or popular.

- Thirdly, live your beliefs. As Romans 1:16 says, we are not to be ashamed of the Gospel. Be the Change you want to see in the world and teach your kids to think the same way by Leading by Example in everything you do.

As parents we also need to instill pride and respect for our county when warranted by:

- Making sure our children know its history

- Treating our military with respect and the honor due them
- Visiting historical sites and monuments to give tangible evidence of our nation's history
- Teach and mirror respect for our flag
- Speak out on matters of Christian principles and morals with resolute truth but with grace and love

God bless America and may The Lord extend His loving grace and mercy to us and give us all the heart and fortitude to work toward restoring the greatness of this land one generation at a time. I truly pray that you and your kids will be part of this moment, not just now but in the continuing generations to follow.

Chapter 9:

Being A Late Bloomer

Everyone wants there kids to be awesome at everything they do all the time but the reality is this will never be the case. Some kids blossom during their elementary school ages, doing great in academics, sports, being one of the most popular kids in school. Other kids bloom later in life during their high school years and win numerous trophies in sports activities, academic competitions, and seem to be that kid that all the other kids want to be.

It's important to understand although we could have touched on these things in our education chapter I feel that is deserves a chapter all to itself. I have touch on younger kids of elementary school age, and I have touch on older high school aged kids but what you may or may not have noticed is that I have not mentioned the middle school aged kids. I wanted to save this group for last and help you to understand as a general rule of thumb as they say these years will be some of the most challenging and very few kids blossom during this time frame. While there are several reasons for this the number one reason is biology.

During these years your child is most likely being effected by a flood of hormones that continue to rush in because of puberty. The best advice I can give you during this time from in a word would be, "Understanding". Understand what your child is going through and give them the love, support, and space to get through it with dignity and grace.

There are times and seasons for everything but the key thing to instill within your child is consistency over the long haul. I strongly believe every child will blossom during some stage in their life, when that is, however, is often not in our control.

Our job as parents is the lead, guide, and protect our kids as best we can with truth, love, and sincerity. We have such as short time to shape the direction of our child's life and thus effect future generations – we cannot take this responsibility lightly. Since you have purchased this book I am confident you are one of those rare parents that understand this reality and will develop into a great parent.

Being a late bloomer is all good

If you find that your child is still struggling with their development and is not progressing as fast as you'd like – Don't sweat it and don't put too much pressure on them. Allow them the number one thing they need to navigate through this life, "The Time to Get to Know Who They Are".

I confess I am partial being a late bloomer myself, but I look back and am so thankful for the way things developed in my life and how my mom gave me the time to really understand who I am without any undo pressure, that would have probably confused the situation even more for me.

Remember there is a time and season under heaven for everything.

"To every thing there is a season, and a time to every purpose under the heaven: A time to be born, and a time to die; a time to plant, and a time to pluck up that which is planted; A time to kill, and a time to heal; a time to break down, and a time to build up; A time to weep, and a time to laugh; a time to mourn, and a time to dance;

A time to cast away stones, and a time to

gather stones together; a time to embrace,

and a time to refrain from embracing; A

time to get, and a time to lose; a time to

keep, and a time to cast away; A time to

rend, and a time to sew; a time to keep

silence, and a time to speak; A time to love,

and a time to hate; a time of war, and a time

of peace" ~ Ecclesiastes 3:1-8, KJV

Chapter 10: Conclusion

It's time for me to wrap this up, but don't worry. You've got this down. You can be an amazing and wonderful parent and example to your children as long as you make Christ the center of your home and of your life without walking in hypocrisy.

I started out by telling you something you already knew—that parenting is both difficult and amazing and that it is the best and hardest job you'll ever have. Hopefully in reading this book you also now have a better grasp of how to make it more wonderful and amazing than it is difficult and hard.

God bless and remember to love your children the way Jesus loves us. – Hold nothing back each day for time is an ever fleeing element that we can never get back. Seize the day!

This book has given you the information you need to be a great parent and raise Awesome kids. I truly hope you have enjoyed this book and have gained some valuable insight to be a great parent and raise awesome kids.

If you have further questions, comments, or would like to stay in touch our contact information can be found at the end of this book. Once again I thank you for your purchase - God Bless.

Special Gift

God has a Gift for You!   The Plan of
Salvation:

There is no formal prayer of salvation as
many churches would have you believe,
God's Word is very clear - there is only one
way to get to the Father in heaven and that is
through Jesus Christ (John 14:6). Jesus says
that you must be born again to enter into
heaven (John 3:3-5).

Salvation is simply the first step in building
an open and honest relationship with God.
We all have sinned and fall short every day,
but there is Hope in Jesus Christ - Just cry
out to God in sincerity and honesty asking
for forgiveness and for Him to Save you,
Sanctify you, and fill you with His Holy
Spirit - Ask for His will to be done in your
life on earth as it is in Heaven and That's it,
now just keep it real with God.

A Warning:

The Christian walk is not an easy life on the surface. The Word of God says that we will be hated in all the world for Christ namesake in the last days (Matt. 24:9). The Bible says that in the last days are enemy prevail against us physically until Christ returns to save us (Dan 7:21, 22). Furthermore, we must endure hardship as a good soldier of Jesus Christ (2 Tim 2:3) and yet we are never alone in this, God promises us that He will never leave us nor forsake us if we believe in Him (Matt.28:20).

In everything we go through we have the peace and joy of God which surpasses all understanding (Philp. 4:6-8) The Bible declares, "For I consider the sufferings of this present time are not worthy to be compared with the glory which shall be revealed in us". (Rom 8:18). However, in all these things we are more than conquerors through Jesus Christ (Rom. 8:37)

Stay In Contact

Our Contact Information

Stay in Contact with the American Christian Defense Alliance, Inc. Contactus@acdainc.org Or Email Us Though Our Website At: www.ACDAInc.Org

Join Our Mailing List

We also Greatly Appreciate You Signing Up For Our Mailing List and Providing a Good Rating and review for this Book. Your reviews help other people like yourself find this book on Amazon and benefit from its contents.

If You or Your Family have been Blessed by this book please let us know by dropping us a line through our website at http://acdainc.org

Thanks Again for Reading - God Bless!

Our Books On Amazon

Some of Our Books on Amazon:

Overcoming 50 Shades of Grey and All the Colors of the LGBT Rainbow: How to Conquer Your Lust and Walk in the Spirit of God

Salvation for Your Unsaved Mom: 10 Things to Tell Your Mom Before She Dies

Real Men Don't Make Promises: Understanding Oaths, Pacts, Covenants & Promises From A Biblical Perspective

The Perfection of Purity: A Message to My Daughter

God's Super Minions: Living Faithfully and Obediently in God

God's Green Smoothie Book: The Naked Truth

Martial Arts Ministry: How To Start A Martial Arts Ministry

Bible Studies for Belts: A Guide for Christian Martial Arts, Vol. 1: White Belt

Christian Prepping 101: How To Start Prepping

How to Finance Your Full-Time RV Dream